~A BINGO BOOK~

The American Civil War Bingo Book

COMPLETE BINGO GAME IN A BOOK

I0167323

Written by Rebecca Stark

© 2016 Barbara M. Peller, also known as Rebecca Stark

The purchase of this book entitles the buyer to exclusive reproduction rights of the student activity pages for his or her class only. The reproduction of any part of the work for an entire school or school system or for commercial use is prohibited.

ISBN 978-0-87386-469-5

Educational Books 'n' Bingo

Printed in the U.S.A.

THE AMERICAN CIVIL WAR BINGO
Directions

INCLUDED:

List of Terms

Templates for Additional Terms and Clues

2 Clues per Term

30 Unique Bingo Cards

Markers

1   **Either cut apart the book or make copies of ALL the sheets. You might want to make an extra copy of the clue sheets to use for introduction and review. Keep the sheets in an envelope for easy reuse.**

2. Cut apart the call cards with terms and clues.

3. Pass out one bingo card per student. There are enough for a class of 30.

4. Pass out markers. You may cut apart the markers included in this book or use any other small items of your choice.

5. Decide whether or not you will require the entire card to be filled. Requiring the entire card to be filled provides a better review. However, if you have a short time to fill, you may prefer to have them do the just the border or some other format. Tell the class before you begin what is required.

6. There are 50 topics. Read the list before you begin. If there are any topics that have not been covered in class, you may want to read to the students the topic and clues before you begin.

7. There is a blank space in the middle of each card. You can instruct the students to use it as a free space or you can write in answers to cover topics not included. Of course, in this case you would create your own clues. (Templates provided.)

8. Shuffle the cards and place them in a pile. Two or three clues are provided for each topic. If you plan to play the game with the same group more than once, you might want to choose a different clue for each game. If not, you may choose to use more than one clue.

9. Be sure to keep the cards you have used for the present game in a separate pile. When a student calls, "Bingo," he or she will have to verify that the correct answers are on his or her card AND that the markers were placed in response to the proper questions. Pull out the cards that are on the student's card keeping them in the order they were used in the game. Read each clue as it was given and ask the student to identify the correct answer from his or her card.

10. If the student has the correct answers on the card AND has shown that they were marked in response to the *correct questions,* then that student is the winner and the game is over. If the student does not have the correct answers on the card OR he or she marked the answers in response to *the wrong questions,* then the game continues until there is a proper winner.

11. If you want to play again, reshuffle the cards and begin again.

Have fun!

                                    © Barbara M. Peller

TERMS INCLUDED

ABOLITIONISTS

ANTIETAM

APPOMATTOX COURT HOUSE

ATLANTA

CLARA BARTON

GENERAL P.G.T BEAUREGARD

BLOCKADE

BORDER STATES

MATHEW B. BRADY

GENERAL BRAXTON BRAGG

JOHN BROWN

BULL RUN

GENERAL AMBROSE BURNSIDE

CARPETBAGGERS

CONFEDERACY

JEFFERSON DAVIS

FREDERICK DOUGLASS

EMANCIPATION PROCLAMATION

FORT SUMTER

GENERAL JOHN CHARLES FRÉMONT

GETTYSBURG

GENERAL ULYSSES S. GRANT

HARPERS FERRY

GENERAL JOSEPH HOOKER

IRONCLADS

GENERAL THOMAS J. JACKSON

GENERAL ROBERT E. LEE

ABRAHAM LINCOLN

GENERAL JAMES LONGSTREET

GENERAL GEORGE B. McCLELLAN

GENERAL GEORGE GORDON MEADE

NULLIFICATION

GENERAL GEORGE E. PICKETT

PLANTATIONS

RECONSTRUCTION

SECESSION

GENERAL PHILIP SHERIDAN

GENERAL WILLIAM SHERMAN

SHILOH

SLAVERY

STATES' RIGHTS

GENERAL "JEB" STUART

TARIFFS

THIRTEENTH AMENDMENT

SOJOURNER TRUTH

HARRIET TUBMAN

UNCLE TOM'S CABIN

UNDERGROUND RAILROAD

UNION

VICKSBURG

© Barbara M. Peller

Additional Terms

Choose as many additional terms as you would like and write them in the squares. Repeat each as desired.
Cut out the squares and randomly distribute them to the class.
Instruct the students to place their square on the center space of their card.

   © Barbara M. Peller

Clues for Additional Terms

Write three clues for each of your additional terms.

_____ 1. 2. 3.	_____ 1. 2. 3.
_____ 1. 2. 3.	_____ 1. 2. 3.
_____ 1. 2. 3.	_____ 1. 2. 3.

© **Barbara M. Peller**

CHARLESTON MERCURY

EXTRA:

THE UNION IS DISSOLVED!

ABOLITIONISTS

1. These people supported the movement to make slavery illegal.
2. They refused to obey laws such as the Fugitive Slave Law, which said free states must return slaves to their owners.
3. William Lloyd Garrison was one who used his newspaper to speak out against slavery.

ANTIETAM

1. This battle in Maryland was the bloodiest *one-day* battle in American history.
2. About 23,000 soldiers were killed, wounded or missing after twelve hours of brutal combat on September 17, 1862.
3. Also known as the Battle of Sharpsburg, it ended the Confederate Army of Northern Virginia's first invasion into the North.

APPOMATTOX COURT HOUSE

1. General Grant formally accepted General Lee's surrender in ___ in Virginia on April 9, 1865.
2. General Joshua Chamberlain was the Union officer selected to lead the ceremony of surrender in this village.
3. General Grant allowed the Confederate soldiers to keep their horses after General Lee's surrender here.

ATLANTA

1. This city in Georgia was used as a center for military operations and as a supply route by the Confederate army during the Civil War.
2. General William Tecumseh Sherman and his troops captured this Southern city in 1864.
3. Union troops burned this to the ground during Sherman's March to the Sea.

CLARA BARTON

1. She is best remembered as the founder of the American Red Cross.
2. She was given a special pass to travel with army ambulances to care for the wounded.
3. She organized a relief effort to get medical supplies after learning that many soldiers had suffered after the First Battle of Bull Run because there were no supplies.

GENERAL P.G.T BEAUREGARD

1. This general opened fire on the Union-held Fort Sumter, starting the American Civil War.
2. With General Joseph E. Johnston, he led Confederate forces to victory in the First Battle of Bull Run.
3. His 2,200-man force resisted an assault by 16,000 Union soldiers in the Second Battle of Petersburg long enough for Lee's army to arrive.

BLOCKADE

1. This is the term for an effort to prevent supplies, troops, or other aid from reaching an enemy.
2. The Union used this means to stop the flow of goods between the South and other countries.
3. Six days after the fall of Fort Sumter, President Lincoln imposed a ___ from South Carolina to Texas and soon extended it to include Virginia and North Carolina.

BORDER STATES

1. This refers to the five slave states that border a free state and sided with the Union: Delaware, Kentucky, Maryland, Missouri, and West Virginia
2. West Virginia was one; it broke away from Virginia because it did not want to secede.
3. Delaware is the only one of the five that does not share a border with a Confederate state.

MATHEW B. BRADY

1. This 19th-century photographer is best known for his documentation of the American Civil War.
2. He is known as the "Father of Photojournalism."
3. His early photographs were daguerreotypes, which were produced on a silver or silver-covered copper plate.

The American Civil War Bingo

GENERAL BRAXTON BRAGG

1. He was victorious at Chickamauga, TN, but failed to take the advice of his generals and did not attack the retreating Union troops.
2. This controversial Confederate general was defeated at the Battle of Chattanooga in Tennessee.
3. In June 1862, he replaced P.G.T. Beauregard as head of the Army of Tennessee.

© Barbara M. Peller

JOHN BROWN
1. This abolitionist advocated and practiced armed insurrection as the means to an end.
2. He attempted to start a liberation movement among enslaved African Americans in Harpers Ferry, Virginia.
3. He was tried for treason against the state of Virginia and was hanged, but many called him a hero.

BULL RUN
1. The first battle here was the first major land battle of the American Civil War.
2. Generals in the second battle here included Pope for the Union and Lee and Jackson for the Confederacy. The Confederates were victorious.
3. There were 22,180 casualties at the second battle here, also called the Second Battle of Manassas.

GENERAL AMBROSE BURNSIDE
1. Lincoln appointed him to command the Army of the Potomac although the general himself felt unqualified.
2. After his defeat at Fredericksburg and his unsuccessful offensive in January 1863, he was replaced as head of the Army of the Potomac.
3. He refused command of the Army of the Potomac twice, citing his inexperience each time.

CARPETBAGGERS
1. This is the term Southerners gave to Northerners who moved to the South during Reconstruction.
2. Southerners did not like them because they considered them ready to loot and plunder the defeated South.
3. Southerners named them for the travel bags they carried.

CONFEDERACY
1. It was formed between 1861 and 1865 by the 11 southern states that seceded from the Union.
2. Its President was Jefferson Davis.
3. For most of its existence, its capital was at Richmond, Virginia.

JEFFERSON DAVIS
1. He was President of the Confederate States of America.
2. After he was captured in 1865, he was charged with treason but never convicted.
3. He met with his Confederate cabinet for the last time on May 5, 1865, and the Confederate Government was officially dissolved.

FREDERICK DOUGLASS
1. This black abolitionist served as an adviser to President Abraham Lincoln during the Civil War.
2. This abolitionist and editor began his life as a slave.
3. This abolitionist changed his last name, which had been Bailey, to make it more difficult for slave catchers to trace him.

EMANCIPATION PROCLAMATION
1. This presidential order declared the freedom of all slaves in the Confederate States.
2. Some people were dissatisfied with this presidential order because it freed slaves only in states over which the Union had no control.
3. This presidential order did not free any slaves in the border states: Kentucky, Missouri, Maryland, Delaware, and West Virginia.

FORT SUMTER
1. The first engagement of the Civil War took place here on April 12 and 13, 1861.
2. The North did not gain control of it until General Sherman's advance through South Carolina forced the Confederates to evacuate Charleston in 1865.
3. This fortification is located in the harbor of Charleston, SC, and was built after the War of 1812 to protect the southern coast.

The American Civil War Bingo

GENERAL JOHN C. FRÉMONT
1. He was nicknamed the "Pathfinder."
2. In the 1840s his expeditions across the Rocky Mountains helped win California from Mexico.
3. As head of the Department of the West, he issued a proclamation declaring martial law in Missouri and ordering secessionists' property to be confiscated and their slaves emancipated. Lincoln revoked this proclamation.

© Barbara M. Peller

GETTYSBURG

1. A battle was fought in this Pennsylvania town from July 1 to July 3. Union victory here ended General Lee's second and most ambitious invasion of the North.
2. ___, Pennsylvania, was the site of the war's bloodiest battle with 51,000 casualties.
3. President Abraham Lincoln gave his most famous address on this battlefield.

GENERAL ULYSSES S. GRANT

1. He was made Commander-in-Chief of the Federal armies in 1864.
2. His campaign ending in the surrender of Vicksburg secured Union control of the Mississippi River.
3. In 1869 he became the eighteenth President of the United States.

HARPERS FERRY

1. This landmark in West Virginia is the site of John Brown's raid.
2. In an effort to seize the 100,000 weapons at the Arsenal, abolitionist John Brown launched his raid here on October 16, 1859.
3. John Brown's raid here failed, but his trial and execution brought the moral issue of slavery to the forefront.

GENERAL JOSEPH HOOKER

1. This Union general was called "Fighting Joe."
2. This Union general was defeated by General Robert E. Lee at the Battle of Chancellorsville in 1863.
3. He became Commander of the Army of the Potomac on January 26, 1863, replacing General Burnside.

IRONCLADS

1. These were developed because of the vulnerability of wooden warships to explosive or incendiary shells.
2. The first battle between ___, the *CSS Virginia* (also known as the *Merrimack*) vs. the *USS Monitor*, took place on March 9, 1862.
3. ___ were high-seas battleships, coastal defense ships, and long-range cruisers.

GENERAL THOMAS J. JACKSON

1. This Confederate general received the nick-name "Stonewall" at the First Battle of Bull Run.
2. This Confederate general fought at the First Battle of Bull Run, the Second Battle of Bull Run, Antietam, and Fredericksburg.
3. He was shot by "friendly fire" at Chancellorsville. His arm was amputated and he died about a week later (May 10, 1863) from pneumonia.

GENERAL ROBERT E. LEE

1. On January 23, 1865, he was named Commander-in-Chief of the Confederate Armies.
2. His greatest victories were the Seven Days Battles, the Second Battle of Bull Run, the Battle of Fredericksburg and the Battle of Chancellorsville.
3. When Johnston was wounded, he was made commander of the Confederate's strongest army, which he renamed the Army of Northern Virginia.

ABRAHAM LINCOLN

1. He was President of the United States during the Civil War.
2. He was assassinated at Ford's Theatre in Washington by John Wilkes Booth, an actor who thought he was helping the South.
3. His most famous speech began, "Four score and twenty years ago our fathers brought forth on this continent a new nation..."

GENERAL JAMES LONGSTREET

1. This Confederate general was known as Lee's Old War Horse and as the Bulldog of Chickamauga.
2. At the Battle of Gettysburg he disagreed with General Lee regarding tactics.
3. He was commander of the Confederate forces during the Seven Days' Campaign.

GENERAL GEORGE B. McCLELLAN

1. He organized the Army of the Potomac and served briefly (November 1861 to March 1862) as the general-in-chief of the Union Army.
2. After the Battle of Antietam, he was ordered to turn over his command to General Burnside.
3. He opposed Lincoln in the 1864 presidential election and ran on an anti-war platform.

The American Civil War Bingo

© **Barbara M. Peller**

GENERAL GEORGE GORDON MEADE

1. This Union general defeated General Robert E. Lee at Gettysburg.
2. Despite the decisive results of the campaign at Gettysburg, he was criticized for the caution he exercised in following Lee's retreat back to Virginia.
3. He replaced General Hooker as commander of the Army of the Potomac.

NULLIFICATION

1. This is the legal theory that a state has the right to nullify, or invalidate, any federal law which that state has deemed unconstitutional.
2. Proponents of this legal theory believed that states could ignore federal acts if they did not approve of them.
3. This assertion that states can ignore federal laws eventually led to secession.

GENERAL GEORGE E. PICKETT

1. This Confederate general is best remembered for his participation in the futile assault at the Battle of Gettysburg that bears his name.
2. His loss at Five Forks to General Sheridan triggered Lee's decision to begin the retreat that led to his surrender.
3. His division was defeated at Five Forks while he was two miles away enjoying a fish bake.

PLANTATIONS

1. These large farms dominated southern agriculture from the mid-18 century to the Civil War.
2. The more slaves the owners of these large farms could work, the greater their output and profits.
3. Cotton became the most important crop on these after the invention of the cotton gin in 1793.

RECONSTRUCTION

1. During this period from the end of the war to 1877 the federal government focused on resolving problems brought about by the Civil War.
2. Issues of ___ were how secessionist states would be reinstated; the status of Confederate leaders; and the status of freed slaves.
3. Amendments 13–15 dealing with slavery and the right to vote were passed during ___.

SECESSION

1. This is the term for the act of withdrawing from an organization, especially a political entity.
2. This action by South Carolina was eventually followed by ten other states
3. This action by eleven states led to the formation of the Confederate States of America.

GENERAL PHILIP SHERIDAN

1. He oversaw the destruction of the Shenandoah Valley, eliminating the Confederate army's major source of food and supplies.
2. His destruction of the economic infrastructure of the Shenandoah Valley was one of the first uses of scorched-earth tactics in the war.
3. In May 1864 his soldiers killed Confederate cavalry leader "Jeb" Stuart at Yellow Tavern.

GENERAL WILLIAM SHERMAN

1. He captured Atlanta on September 2, 1864, and ordered the burning of its military and government buildings.
2. His "March to the Sea" ended with the capture of Savannah on December 22, 1864.
3. Before burning Atlanta's military and government buildings, he ordered civilians to leave the city.

SHILOH

1. This major battle in the Western Theater is also known as the Battle of Pittsburgh Landing.
2. Confederate forces under Generals Johnston and Beauregard launched a surprise attack here and almost defeated Union Army of General Grant.
3. Reinforcements from General Buell turned the tide of this battle and Buell and Grant launched a counterattack, forcing the Confederates to retreat.

SLAVERY

1. The legal end to it in the United States came in December 1865 when the Thirteenth Amendment was ratified.
2. This was a factor in the debate about the annexation of Texas in 1865.
3. Two attempts to deal with this issue before the war were the Missouri Compromise (1820–21) and the Compromise of 1850.

The American Civil War Bingo

© Barbara M. Peller

STATES' RIGHTS 1. Secession was based on this idea that the powers of the individual states were greater than those of the federal government. 2. Regarding this issue, the South wanted all undefined powers to be reserved for the individual states. 3. Regarding this issue, the North wanted the federal government to have expanded powers.	**GENERAL "JEB" STUART** 1. He and three of his brigades were separated from Lee's army during the approach and first two days of the Battle of Gettysburg. 2. In 1864 he was defeated by General Philip Sheridan during the Overland Campaign. 3. This Confederate cavalryman was killed during the Battle of Yellow Tavern during the Overland Campaign.
TARIFFS 1. One quarrel between the North and the South was because of these taxes that were paid on goods from foreign countries. 2. Southerners felt these were unfair because they imported more goods than the Northerners. 3. The South opposed ____ because Southern goods shipped to foreign countries were taxed but Northern goods of weren't always taxed.	**THIRTEENTH AMENDMENT** 1.This abolished and prohibited slavery and involuntary servitude in the entire United States. 2. After the war but before its ratification, slavery remained legal only in Delaware, Kentucky, Missouri, Maryland, and West Virginia. 3. It made an exception to the prohibition of involuntary servitude for those duly convicted of a crime.
SOJOURNER TRUTH 1. This was name taken by Isabella Baumfree, an abolitionist and women's rights activist. 2. Her speech "Ain't I a Woman?" was delivered in 1851 at the Ohio Women's Rights Convention. 3. When she became a travelling preacher, abolitionist and women's-rights activist Isabella Baumfree changed her name to this.	**HARRIET TUBMAN** 1. During a 10-year span as a "conductor" of the Underground Railroad, this runaway slave helped more than 300 slaves escape. 2. She risked her life to help others escape by way of the Underground Railroad and said she never lost a "passenger." 3. She was called "Grandma Moses" because she led so many people to freedom.
UNCLE TOM'S CABIN 1. This anti-slavery novel was written by Harriet Beecher Stowe. 2. This novel depicts the cruel reality of slavery and helped increase anti-slavery sentiments. 3. Although this book did a great deal to help the abolitionist cause and was a great tool against slavery, it also created many stereotypes about blacks.	**UNDERGROUND RAILROAD** 1. This vast network of people helped runaway slaves escape to the North and to Canada. 2. Harriet Tubman was its most famous "conductor." 3. This organized system of freeing slaves began in 1780, but was not given this name until about 1831 when steam railroads were emerging.
UNION 1. This name was often used to signify the North during the American Civil War. 2. This name was sometimes used to refer to all 23 states which were not part of the seceding Confederacy. 3. West Virginia separated from Virginia and became part of this during the war.	**VICKSBURG** 1. The surrender of this city along with the fall of Port Hudson, LA, divided the South and gave the North undisputed control of the Mississippi. 2. General Pemberton formally surrendered control of this city in Mississippi to General Grant on July 4, 1863. 3. Grant's campaign against this city in Mississippi lasted from May 18 to July 4, 1863.

The American Civil War Bingo

© Barbara M. Peller

The American Civil War Bingo

Frederick Douglass	Abolitionists	General P.G.T. Beauregard	General Joseph Hooker	General James Longstreet
Blockade	Antietam	Harriet Tubman	General George G. Meade	Underground Railroad
Appomattox Court House	Vicksburg		Plantations	General Braxton Bragg
General "Jeb" Stuart	Jefferson Davis	Union	General Thomas J. Jackson	General George E. Pickett
Secession	General John C. Frémont	Slavery	Uncle Tom's Cabin	Thirteenth Amendment

     © Barbara M. Peller

The American Civil War Bingo

General "Jeb" Stuart	Appomattox Court House	General George B. McClellan	Tariffs	Harpers Ferry
General George E. Pickett	General Ambrose Burnside	Atlanta	Border States	General Robert E. Lee
Bull Run	General John C. Frémont		Emancipation Proclamation	Union
General William Sherman	Reconstruction	Vicksburg	Shiloh	Thirteenth Amendment
Underground Railroad	Harriet Tubman	Slavery	Blockade	Uncle Tom's Cabin

© Barbara M. Peller

The American Civil War Bingo

General "Jeb" Stuart	Union	General Ambrose Burnside	General Thomas J. Jackson	Appomattox Court House
General George G. Meade	Antietam	John Brown	Abolitionists	Border States
Jefferson Davis	Harriet Tubman		General Robert E. Lee	Clara Barton
Vicksburg	Bull Run	Secession	General William Sherman	General George B. McClellan
Uncle Tom's Cabin	Blockade	Slavery	Shiloh	Harpers Ferry

 © Barbara M. Peller

The American Civil War Bingo

Vicksburg	General Robert E. Lee	General P.G.T. Beauregard	Border States	Harpers Ferry
Abraham Lincoln	Mathew B. Brady	Abolitionists	Tariffs	Appomattox Court House
Plantations	General William Sherman		General James Longstreet	General Joseph Hooker
Union	Carpetbaggers	Harriet Tubman	Slavery	Atlanta
Border States	Underground Railroad	Reconstruction	Uncle Tom's Cabin	General Braxton Bragg

© Barbara M. Peller

The American Civil War Bingo

Underground Railroad	General James Longstreet	Jefferson Davis	Atlanta	Blockade
Abraham Lincoln	Union	John Brown	Emancipation Proclamation	Antietam
General P.G.T. Beauregard	General Braxton Bragg		General George G. Meade	Gettysburg
Thirteenth Amendment	Harpers Ferry	Frederick Douglass	Shiloh	Confederacy
General Ambrose Burnside	Slavery	Appomattox Court House	Vicksburg	Plantations

© Barbara M. Peller

The American Civil War Bingo

Clara Barton	General Robert E. Lee	General George B. McClellan	Harpers Ferry	General Braxton Bragg
General Thomas J. Jackson	Jefferson Davis	Confederacy	Abolitionists	Appomattox Court House
Tariffs	Border States		Mathew B. Brady	Emancipation Proclamation
Slavery	Secession	Shiloh	Reconstruction	General P.G.T. Beauregard
General George E. Pickett	Atlanta	Frederick Douglass	Plantations	Carpetbaggers

 © Barbara M. Peller

The American Civil War Bingo

Frederick Douglass	General Robert E. Lee	Gettysburg	General George G. Meade	General Ambrose Burnside
General George E. Pickett	Harpers Ferry	General John C. Frémont	Antietam	Abraham Lincoln
General George B. McClellan	General Joseph Hooker		Emancipation Proclamation	Mathew B. Brady
Vicksburg	General William Sherman	John Brown	General "Jeb" Stuart	Bull Run
Slavery	Blockade	Shiloh	Reconstruction	Clara Barton

© Barbara M. Peller

The American Civil War Bingo

Plantations	General Robert E. Lee	Fort Sumter	General Thomas J. Jackson	Mathew B. Brady
Abraham Lincoln	General P.G.T. Beauregard	Tariffs	General Braxton Bragg	Atlanta
Carpetbaggers	General Philip Sheridan		Harpers Ferry	General James Longstreet
Uncle Tom's Cabin	Vicksburg	General "Jeb" Stuart	Border States	General William Sherman
Harriet Tubman	Slavery	Reconstruction	Jefferson Davis	General George E. Pickett

© Barbara M. Peller

The American Civil War Bingo

Emancipation Proclamation	General Ambrose Burnside	General John C. Frémont	Carpetbaggers	Blockade
Border States	Harpers Ferry	Plantations	Jefferson Davis	General Robert E. Lee
Ironclads	Frederick Douglass		Antietam	Fort Sumter
Confederacy	Thirteenth Amendment	Secession	General George G. Meade	Gettysburg
General William Sherman	Shiloh	John Brown	General "Jeb" Stuart	General James Longstreet

© Barbara M. Peller

The American Civil War Bingo

General "Jeb" Stuart	General Thomas J. Jackson	Mathew B. Brady	Tariffs	Carpetbaggers
General Braxton Bragg	Atlanta	Abolitionists	Antietam	Harpers Ferry
General Philip Sheridan	General Robert E. Lee		General Joseph Hooker	Bull Run
Secession	Thirteenth Amendment	Confederacy	Shiloh	Ironclads
John Brown	General George E. Pickett	General George B. McClellan	Underground Railroad	Plantations

 © Barbara M. Peller

The American Civil War Bingo

Clara Barton	General Robert E. Lee	Jefferson Davis	Confederacy	General George E. Pickett
Fort Sumter	Ironclads	General George G. Meade	Emancipation Proclamation	Abolitionists
Abraham Lincoln	Harpers Ferry		General George B. McClellan	General John C. Frémont
John Brown	States' Rights	Shiloh	Blockade	General "Jeb" Stuart
Border States	Slavery	Frederick Douglass	Reconstruction	General Ambrose Burnside

© Barbara M. Peller

The American Civil War Bingo

General Ambrose Burnside	General James Longstreet	Ironclads	General Thomas J. Jackson	Emancipation Proclamation
General John C. Frémont	General George E. Pickett	General P.G.T. Beauregard	Reconstruction	Antietam
Frederick Douglass	Gettysburg		General Braxton Bragg	Tariffs
Slavery	General William Sherman	Harpers Ferry	General "Jeb" Stuart	Abraham Lincoln
General Robert E. Lee	Fort Sumter	General Philip Sheridan	Border States	Atlanta

© Barbara M. Peller

The American Civil War Bingo

Confederacy	General James Longstreet	Clara Barton	Ironclads	General Braxton Bragg
General P.G.T. Beauregard	Fort Sumter	Harpers Ferry	Emancipation Proclamation	Bull Run
General Thomas J. Jackson	General Ambrose Burnside		General John C. Frémont	Gettysburg
Plantations	Shiloh	Mathew B. Brady	General Philip Sheridan	General "Jeb" Stuart
Slavery	Thirteenth Amendment	Reconstruction	Frederick Douglass	General George G. Meade

© Barbara M. Peller

The American Civil War Bingo

Blockade	Harpers Ferry	Jefferson Davis	Emancipation Proclamation	Border States
Atlanta	Frederick Douglass	Ironclads	Antietam	General Robert E. Lee
Confederacy	General Joseph Hooker		General George B. McClellan	John Brown
Thirteenth Amendment	Shiloh	General Philip Sheridan	Mathew B. Brady	Clara Barton
Slavery	Tariffs	Bull Run	General George E. Pickett	Plantations

    © Barbara M. Peller

The American Civil War Bingo

General George G. Meade	Emancipation Proclamation	Jefferson Davis	General Ambrose Burnside	General Thomas J. Jackson
Clara Barton	General George B. McClellan	Abolitionists	General P.G.T. Beauregard	Border States
General Braxton Bragg	Frederick Douglass		Appomattox Court House	General Robert E. Lee
Slavery	Ironclads	Fort Sumter	Shiloh	Confederacy
General George E. Pickett	General William Sherman	Reconstruction	Carpetbaggers	General John C. Frémont

© Barbara M. Peller

The American Civil War Bingo

Mathew B. Brady	Ironclads	Fort Sumter	Carpetbaggers	Border States
Tariffs	Bull Run	Gettysburg	Abraham Lincoln	General Joseph Hooker
Confederacy	General James Longstreet		General Braxton Bragg	General John C. Frémont
Vicksburg	Atlanta	Slavery	Nullification	General "Jeb" Stuart
States' Rights	Sojourner Truth	Reconstruction	General William Sherman	General Robert E. Lee

© Barbara M. Peller

The American Civil War Bingo

John Brown	Nullification	General Ulysses S. Grant	Ironclads	Blockade
General George G. Meade	Border States	Shiloh	General Joseph Hooker	Gettysburg
Emancipation Proclamation	Plantations		Sojourner Truth	Fort Sumter
Thirteenth Amendment	General George E. Pickett	General "Jeb" Stuart	Jefferson Davis	Bull Run
Secession	Confederacy	General Ambrose Burnside	General Thomas J. Jackson	General James Longstreet

© Barbara M. Peller

The American Civil War Bingo

Carpetbaggers	General Philip Sheridan	Atlanta	Confederacy	Tariffs
General Robert E. Lee	John Brown	Secession	General Braxton Bragg	Border States
Emancipation Proclamation	Bull Run		General Ulysses S. Grant	General P.G.T. Beauregard
Thirteenth Amendment	Abolitionists	Shiloh	General "Jeb" Stuart	General George B. McClellan
Sojourner Truth	Ironclads	Jefferson Davis	Clara Barton	Nullification

© Barbara M. Peller

The American Civil War Bingo

General Braxton Bragg	Clara Barton	Ironclads	Fort Sumter	General Braxton Bragg
General George G. Meade	General Thomas J. Jackson	General Robert E. Lee	General Ambrose Burnside	General Joseph Hooker
Nullification	Blockade		Antietam	Appomattox Court House
General George B. McClellan	Sojourner Truth	Secession	General William Sherman	General Ulysses S. Grant
General P.G.T. Beauregard	States' Rights	General George E. Pickett	Plantations	Reconstruction

© Barbara M. Peller

The American Civil War Bingo

General Philip Sheridan	Nullification	General Thomas J. Jackson	Ironclads	Reconstruction
Atlanta	General John C. Frémont	Abraham Lincoln	Secession	Tariffs
General James Longstreet	Gettysburg		Vicksburg	Abolitionists
Underground Railroad	Harriet Tubman	Uncle Tom's Cabin	General William Sherman	Sojourner Truth
Union	Plantations	States' Rights	General "Jeb" Stuart	General Ulysses S. Grant

     © Barbara M. Peller

The American Civil War Bingo

General George G. Meade	Clara Barton	Abraham Lincoln	Ironclads	Underground Railroad
General James Longstreet	General Ulysses S. Grant	Mathew B. Brady	Fort Sumter	Frederick Douglass
Bull Run	General George E. Pickett		Nullification	Jefferson Davis
Secession	General Ambrose Burnside	Sojourner Truth	Thirteenth Amendment	Plantations
Vicksburg	States' Rights	Reconstruction	John Brown	General William Sherman

© Barbara M. Peller

The American Civil War Bingo

Carpetbaggers	General George B. McClellan	General Ulysses S. Grant	General P.G.T. Beauregard	Confederacy
Tariffs	General Thomas J. Jackson	Appomattox Court House	Fort Sumter	Antietam
Atlanta	General Joseph Hooker		Frederick Douglass	Gettysburg
Sojourner Truth	Thirteenth Amendment	General William Sherman	Abolitionists	Blockade
States' Rights	John Brown	Nullification	Bull Run	Abraham Lincoln

© Barbara M. Peller

The American Civil War Bingo

Mathew B. Brady	Nullification	General Ambrose Burnside	General P.G.T. Beauregard	Reconstruction
Clara Barton	General Philip Sheridan	General George E. Pickett	General George G. Meade	Abolitionists
General George B. McClellan	Confederacy		Uncle Tom's Cabin	Frederick Douglass
Bull Run	States' Rights	Sojourner Truth	John Brown	General William Sherman
Underground Railroad	Harriet Tubman	Plantations	Secession	General Ulysses S. Grant

© Barbara M. Peller

The American Civil War Bingo

Mathew B. Brady	General Philip Sheridan	Blockade	Nullification	Fort Sumter
General Ulysses S. Grant	Reconstruction	Abraham Lincoln	Tariffs	Frederick Douglass
Gettysburg	Carpetbaggers		Confederacy	Bull Run
Underground Railroad	Uncle Tom's Cabin	Sojourner Truth	John Brown	General James Longstreet
Union	Vicksburg	States' Rights	General Thomas J. Jackson	Harriet Tubman

© Barbara M. Peller

The American Civil War Bingo

Vicksburg	Abraham Lincoln	Nullification	Jefferson Davis	General Ulysses S. Grant
Abolitionists	Thirteenth Amendment	General George G. Meade	Mathew B. Brady	Antietam
General James Longstreet	Fort Sumter		Uncle Tom's Cabin	Sojourner Truth
Appomattox Court House	Underground Railroad	Harriet Tubman	States' Rights	General Joseph Hooker
Reconstruction	Blockade	Atlanta	Border States	Union

© Barbara M. Peller

The American Civil War Bingo

General Ulysses S. Grant	Nullification	General George B. McClellan	Tariffs	Carpetbaggers
Secession	General Thomas J. Jackson	Fort Sumter	General Philip Sheridan	Mathew B. Brady
Thirteenth Amendment	Uncle Tom's Cabin		General Joseph Hooker	Vicksburg
John Brown	General P.G.T. Beauregard	Underground Railroad	States' Rights	Sojourner Truth
Gettysburg	Border States	Jefferson Davis	Harriet Tubman	Union

© Barbara M. Peller

The American Civil War Bingo

General George B. McClellan	Atlanta	Nullification	General Philip Sheridan	General John C. Frémont
Underground Railroad	Uncle Tom's Cabin	General George G. Meade	Sojourner Truth	Antietam
Shiloh	Harriet Tubman		States' Rights	Vicksburg
Carpetbaggers	Clara Barton	Abraham Lincoln	Union	Abolitionists
Border States	General Joseph Hooker	General Ulysses S. Grant	Appomattox Court House	Gettysburg

© Barbara M. Peller

The American Civil War Bingo

General Braxton Bragg	General Philip Sheridan	Appomattox Court House	Nullification	Mathew B. Brady
General John C. Frémont	General Ulysses S. Grant	Uncle Tom's Cabin	Tariffs	General Joseph Hooker
Harriet Tubman	Bull Run		Gettysburg	Secession
General "Jeb" Stuart	Carpetbaggers	General George E. Pickett	States' Rights	Sojourner Truth
General P.G.T. Beauregard	Emancipation Proclamation	Border States	Union	Underground Railroad

© Barbara M. Peller

The American Civil War Bingo

General Ulysses S. Grant	General Philip Sheridan	Carpetbaggers	General George G. Meade	Emancipation Proclamation
Thirteenth Amendment	Secession	Abraham Lincoln	Gettysburg	Appomattox Court House
General James Longstreet	Uncle Tom's Cabin		Antietam	Nullification
Jefferson Davis	Underground Railroad	Harpers Ferry	States' Rights	Sojourner Truth
Border States	Fort Sumter	Union	Clara Barton	Harriet Tubman

© Barbara M. Peller

The American Civil War Bingo

Blockade	Nullification	Tariffs	Emancipation Proclamation	Sojourner Truth
Abolitionists	General Philip Sheridan	General George B. McClellan	General Joseph Hooker	Antietam
Thirteenth Amendment	Confederacy		Gettysburg	Abraham Lincoln
Union	Clara Barton	General P.G.T. Beauregard	States' Rights	Uncle Tom's Cabin
Underground Railroad	General Ambrose Burnside	Harriet Tubman	General Ulysses S. Grant	Appomattox Court House

© Barbara M. Peller

www.ingramcontent.com/pod-product-compliance
Lightning Source LLC
La Vergne TN
LVHW061339060426
835511LV00014B/2007